I'M THE
BIGGEST!

IN THE ARCTIC

LAURA K. MURRAY

CREATIVE EDUCATION   CREATIVE PAPERBACKS

CONT

LET'S EXPLORE THE ARCTIC!

The air is cold and dry. Use your binoculars to peer across the ice. A huge polar bear lumbers near the open water. It is hunting for seals.

Frozen Tundra

The Arctic **tundra** contains a layer of frozen soil called permafrost. Permafrost may be more than 1,000 feet (305 m) thick. A thinner layer of soil lies above the permafrost. This layer thaws each summer.

tundra - a flat, treeless region that contains a layer of permafrost, or permanently frozen soil

Sea ice is important to Arctic life and Earth's oceans. But there is less sea ice today than 30 years ago. It forms when ocean water freezes. Sea ice melts each summer. It refreezes in the fall.

1988

2.5 million square miles

2017

1.6 million square miles

Two Months to Grow

The tundra has a shorter growing season than warmer places. It lasts only 60 days. Trees and other large plants cannot grow because of the cold temperatures and thick permafrost.

Winter

Spring

Summer

Fall

growing season

Arctic willow
6 inches (15.2 cm) tall

Shrubs such as the Arctic willow have shallow roots. They grow closer to the ground than trees. This helps them endure the cold and windy conditions. **Lichens** (*LIE-kins*) grow over the ground and rocks. Their small size helps them survive.

lichens - slow-growing organisms made up of fungi and algae

Animals, Big and Small

Bowhead whales are some of the largest Arctic animals. They can grow to 60 feet (18.3 m) long. They may weigh 200,000 pounds (90,718 kg). Bowhead whales have the biggest mouths on Earth. Their **baleen** can be 14 feet (4.3 m) long!

baleen - parts in a whale's mouth that filter food out of seawater

size comparison

weight comparison
~ empty space shuttle

carnivores - animals that eat meat

Polar bears are smaller than bowhead whales. But they are the world's biggest land **carnivores**. Tiny **phytoplankton** flourish when sea ice melts. Many Arctic animals eat phytoplankton.

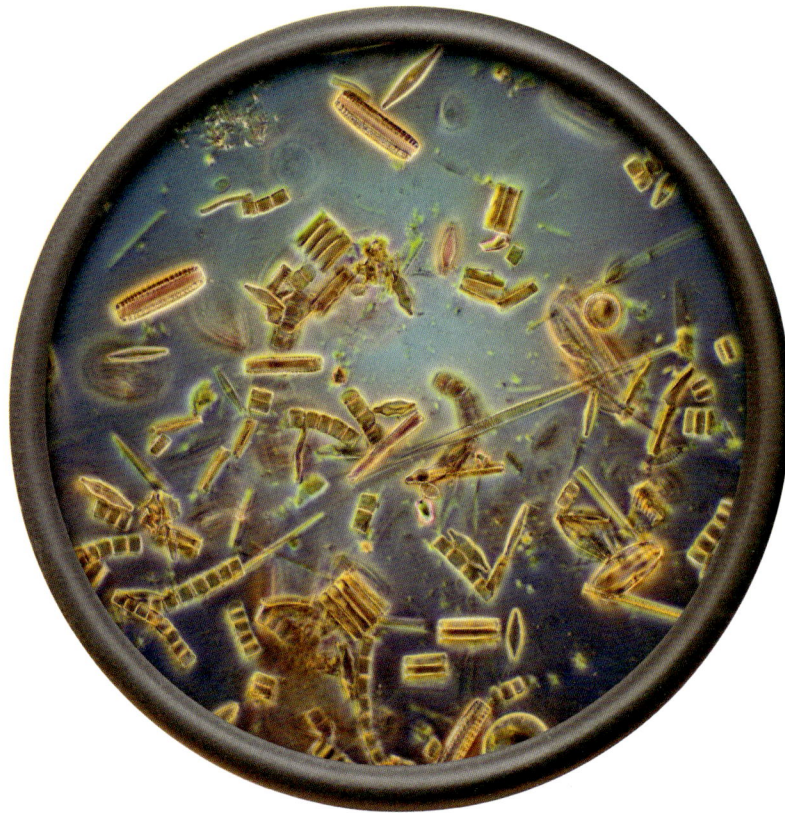

Full of Life

From phytoplankton to bowhead whales, the Arctic is full of life. What other amazing things can you discover about this cold, northern place?

tundra wolf

Arctic fox

snowy owl

polar bear

caribou

Arctic tundra region

Antarctic tundra region

IN THE
ARCTIC

Continents with greatest areas of Arctic tundra:

3 Europe

2 Asia

1 North America

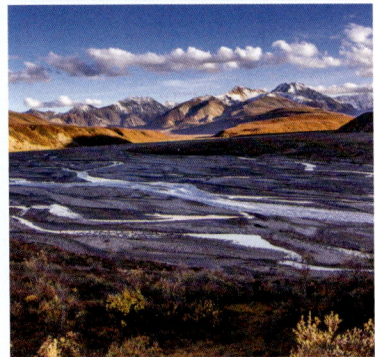

Word Review

Do you remember what these words mean? Look at the pictures for clues, and go back to the page where the words were defined, if you need help.

baleen page 14

carnivores page 16

lichens page 13

phytoplankton page 17

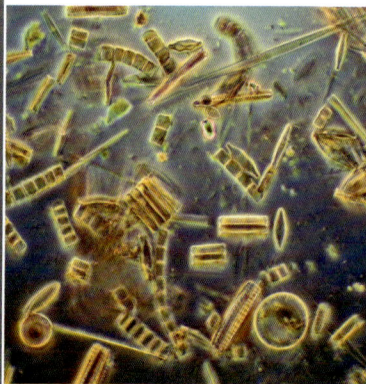

tundra page 7

Read More

Pettiford, Rebecca. *Arctic Food Chains: Who Eats What?*
Minneapolis: Jump!, 2016.

Trueit, Trudi Strain. *Polar Bears.*
North Mankato, Minn.: Amicus, 2016.

Websites

NASA Climate Kids: Winners and Losers in the Arctic

https://climatekids.nasa.gov/arctic-animals/

Read an article about climate change in the Arctic.

National Geographic Kids: Arctic Animal Memory

http://kids.nationalgeographic.com/games/quick-play/arctic-animal-memory/

Play a memory game about Arctic animals.

Index

PUBLISHED BY CREATIVE EDUCATION AND CREATIVE PAPERBACKS
P.O. Box 227, Mankato, Minnesota 56002
Creative Education and Creative Paperbacks
are imprints of The Creative Company
www.thecreativecompany.us

LIBRARY OF CONGRESS CATALOGING-IN-PUBLICATION DATA
Names: Murray, Laura K., author.
Title: In the Arctic / Laura K. Murray.
Series: I'm the biggest.
Summary: From shortest to longest and biggest to smallest, this ecosystem investigation uses varying degrees of comparison to take a closer look at the relationships of the Arctic's flora, fauna, and landforms.

Identifiers: ISBN 978-1-64026-059-7 (hardcover) / ISBN 978-1-62832-647-5 (pbk) / ISBN 978-1-64000-175-6 (eBook)
This title has been submitted for CIP processing under LCCN 2018938951.

CCSS: RI.1.1, 2, 4, 5, 6, 7; RI.2.1, 2, 5, 6, 7; RI.3.1, 2, 5, 7; RF.1.1, 3, 4; RF.2.3, 4

DESIGN AND PRODUCTION
by Joe Kahnke; art direction by Rita Marshall
Printed in the United States of America

PHOTOGRAPHS by Alamy (Ashley Cooper, louise murray, Scenics & Science), FreeVectorMaps.com, Getty Images (Frank Lukasseck/Photographer's Choice, Anton Petrus/Moment, Jeff Vanuga/Corbis), iStockphoto (cliffwass, goinyk, HaizhanZheng, Mario_Hoppmann, JackF, jocrebbin, mmac72, Nick_Pandevonium, roberthyrons, SeppFriedhuber), National Geographic Creative (PAUL NICKLEN), Shutterstock (ILYA AKINSHIN, blojfo, Iakov Filimonov, Volodymyr Goinyk, aleksander hunta, Ice_AisberG, Eric Isselee, Dmitry Kalinovsky, KenshiDesign, Kristina Ponomareva, Jim H Walling, yevgeniy11)

FIRST EDITION HC 9 8 7 6 5 4 3 2 1
FIRST EDITION PBK 9 8 7 6 5 4 3 2 1